THE CURIOUS
BARTENDER'S
HOME BAR GUIDE

THE CURIOUS

BARTENDER'S

HOME BAR GUIDE

Become a master of mixology with expert instruction on how to
set up your home bar and create the perfect drink every time

TRISTAN STEPHENSON

RYLAND PETERS & SMALL
LONDON • NEW YORK

Designer Paul Stradling (based on an original design concept by Geoff Borin)
Editors Nathan Joyce and Gillian Haslam
Picture Researcher Christina Borsi
Art Director Leslie Harrington
Editorial Director Julia Charles
Production Controller David Hearn
Publisher Cindy Richards

Indexer Hilary Bird

Published in 2017 by
Ryland Peters & Small
20–21 Jockey's Fields
London WC1R 4BW
and
341 East 116th Street
New York, NY 10029

www.rylandpeters.com

ISBN for kit 978-1-84975-897-0

10 9 8 7 6 5 4 3 2 1

Printed in China

CONTENTS

— ◆ —

INTRODUCTION

◆

I enjoy having friends over for dinner, but must confess that I rarely make cocktails for my guests. I think this comes as a surprise to some of them, who (quite rightly) expect someone who has made a living from mixing drinks to be mixing martinis on a nightly basis. There are two reasons why I don't make drinks at home very often: the first is that I drink enough cocktails in my bars as it is, and sometimes it's nice to just crack open a bottle of wine and sit back; the second reason has more worrying implications, as it's for the simple fact that I find mixing drinks at home a bit of a chore.

With that little revelation, you might be wondering how this book is going to teach you to become a kitchen cocktail hero, when the person writing the book – the person who has made hundreds of thousands of cocktails over the past two decades – finds it too strenuous a task to shake a cocktail for his own wife.

The problem is that I, like pretty much everyone else on the planet, have never been taught how to make good drinks at home. I was taught to bartend. In a bar. But a professional bar station and a domestic kitchen have very little in common with one another. Asking a top bartender to make world-class drinks at home is no easier than expecting a Michelin star chef to produce a tasting menu from scratch in a domestic kitchen. It's not impossible but it requires a transfer of skill to a different environment, using and sometimes substituting equipment, and doing all of it in what is generally a far more confined space.

A change of tack is required, but for a professional bartender it can be a difficult transition to make. To shake off years of training and gained experience and to start all over again with low work tops, no ice-well, and an inefficient arrangement of bins, sinks, and fridges. But for someone who has never worked in a bar, and who has never experienced what it's like to be 'five deep in the weeds' at 11pm on a Saturday night, learning to bartend in a kitchen is not a great challenge at all. And in some respects your kitchen is already fairly well set up for mixing drinks: you have running water, a freezer, plenty of ingredients, and a wealth of utensils.

The secret, then, lies in practice and preparation; understanding what you're going to need, when you will need it, and how best to make ready for it. As with cooking, it's entirely possible to produce something delicious and to make an incredible mess at the same time. But unlike cooking, your guests will not be content with seeing a tray laden with beautiful cocktails floating into the room as you kick the door shut and hide a scene of complete devastation in the kitchen. One of the great and curious things about mixing drinks is finding that your friends and family want to witness and comment on the making process. Cocktails are about seeing the motion of the bartender, and witnessing the picking, pouring and stirring of ingredients to a perfect state.

In summary, there are two things that I hope you, dear reader, will take from this book: the first is to understand what equipment and ingredients you need to use or source. Second is to understand the basic techniques you need to master to get the best out of the ingredients and to look like a pro at the same time. The accompanying cocktail recipe cards will put all of this into practice, elevating your status to expert level and helping you to select the ideal cocktail for any occasion.

EQUIPMENT & ESSENTIALS

◆

These days there are virtually no limits to the range and variety of bar equipment available to the bartender and home enthusiast. The world's great cocktail bars regularly call for expensive equipment to make their drinks and this builds upon the theatre of the experience, adding value to your evening and validating the cash it costs you. At home, however, a vintage gold-plated cocktail shaker is a luxury that most of us cannot afford and that absolutely none of us need.

So let's set the record straight from the start: you don't need lots of fancy equipment to make great drinks at home. All of the drinks featured in this kit can be produced with nothing more than the included jigger, a cocktail shaker, bar spoon and a good supply of ice. And even a cocktail shaker can be substituted for a plastic container with a lid or a jam jar, the bar spoon swapped for a dessert spoon, and a sieve used in place of a bartender's hawthorn strainer. The notion that a cocktail is indulgent and worthy of respect is not something that I think should be challenged, but behind closed kitchen doors nobody cares how elegant the process of making them is. Indeed, as a professional bartender I have travelled the world with little more than a jigger, beaker, spoon and glass, and still managed to knock together some crowd-pleasing cocktails when the circumstances required me to.

Limes don't have to be squeezed with a fancy geared citrus press (also known as a Mexican elbow), and instead of silver ice tongs, any combination of finger and thumb will suffice. When bartending on shift I will, of course, present drinks using the arsenal of tools available to me, but when making a nightcap at home you had best believe that I often utilise some unconventional equipment to achieve common bartending tasks, and it's not unusual to see me working by the light of the open fridge door.

Here is a list of the most common bartending equipment and their uses.

JIGGER

If you bought this kit, you already have this base well covered. The jigger is the most important utensil in the home bartender's arsenal as it allows you to measure ingredients accurately. Doesn't sound like much fun, does it? Perhaps not, but inaccuracy causes imbalance and imbalance is the root of all evil where cocktails are concerned. Get used to thinking about measurements (in millilitres, or in ounces if you really

must) but more than that, get used to thinking about ratios – 'two parts of this, one part of that.' Where a drink has more than five ingredients this can become tricky, but approaching each drink as a ratio of ingredients rather than a sum of numbers will be useful if you've misplaced your jigger and for when you need double, triple or quadruple quantities. Once you have ratios mastered, you'll find that an egg cup or shot glass can function nicely as a stand-in jigger.

BAR SPOON

Probably the second most important piece of kit ('huh, but what about the shaker?!'), a bar spoon is basically a weighted teaspoon with a long, usually twisted, shaft. Bar spoons are useful for a variety of tasks, the most obvious of which is stirring. Since stirred cocktails require quite a lot of ice, a conventional teaspoon is far too short to reach the bottom of the glass. A dessert or tablespoon is too

cumbersome to achieve the required level of gentle manipulation, so that really only leaves you with a bar spoon. Except, of course, for the fact that a pair of chopsticks also does quite a good job of stirring ice in a tall beaker or glass. In fact, I have found that they are better suited than most bar spoons. Of course you can't spoon ingredients using chopsticks, which brings us on to the second function of a bar spoon: measuring.

Bar spoons are generally quite unreliable when it comes to measuring. The bowl of the spoon varies in volume between brands, but generally sits somewhere between 5 and 10 ml (or the equivalent of 1 and 2 teaspoons). The bigger problem lies in the fact that a 'full' measure from a bar spoon varies from person to person and from pour to pour, ranging from a meagre droplet to a wobbly daub of liquid barely held together by a thin meniscus. In my opinion, it's far better to use your jigger for small measures and keep the bar spoon for what it's best at.

There are a couple of other uses for a bar spoon. The ones with a flat, coin-like piece on the end are designed to assist with floating or layering ingredients in cocktails that call for it – Irish Coffee, for example. The idea is that you rest the base of the spoon on the surface of the drink, then pour the ingredient that is to be floated down the spiral shaft of the spoon. The shaft slows the descent of the liquid by twisting it around and the base disperses it evenly over the surface of the drink. The situations that call for such a trick are few and far between however, so I wouldn't go out and buy a spoon for this reason alone.

That flat base can also be used in place of a muddler (see page 16) to squash soft fruit or bruise herbs. Beware though – I have seen glasses smashed and hands scarred in the engagement in activities such as these. Do it only as a last resort.

EQUIPMENT & ESSENTIALS

SHAKER

Most shakers are made from stainless steel and are comprised of either a steel 'tin' and 'boston' glass, or of a tin with clip-on strainer and cap known as a 'three-piece' shaker. There are positives and negatives to both designs: the boston tends to hold more liquid and has the benefit of a glass so you have an idea of what you've put in there (and what you haven't). The glass part also means it's breakable and the design means that you need a strainer of some sort to stop the ice from flooding out when you pour the drink. The three-piece is a self-contained unit with a strainer built in, but these shakers tend to suffer from being a bit small – for my appetite, at least. A large plastic three-piece is rather surprisingly the best solution: virtually unbreakable, easy to clean, and a good insulator of temperature, meaning that your drinks will get colder quicker and with less dilution of flavour.

MIXING BEAKER

This is a large, open-top vessel used for stirring drinks. Any shaker can serve the purpose, but I think it's sometimes nice to stir drinks down in a lipped glass and watch as the corners of the ice cubes round off as the drink chills. If a mixing beaker sounds a lot like a small jug or pitcher to you, you're not wrong at all. The only difference is they tend not to have handles.

STRAINERS

Hawthorn strainers are comprised of a perforated metal plate with a coil of wire running around the edge and they sit over the top of a cocktail tin when pouring, so as to hold all the ice back. They are essential if you're shaking cocktails with a boston shaker, but surplus to requirements if it's a three-piece that is your thing.

Another type of strainer is a julep strainer. These are like large perforated spoons that were originally designed to stop ice from falling in your face when sipping on a Mint Julep. They're unsuitable for straining shaken drinks as the holes either get blocked or let too much ice through, but some bartenders like to use them for straining stirred cocktails where there is little risk of tiny ice fragments ending up in the glass.

The final type of strainer, which there's a good chance you have already, is a tea strainer, a.k.a. a small sieve. Finer (smaller holes) is better where these things are concerned, as tea strainers are used as a secondary strain when pouring some shaken drinks as a means of keeping the fine ice shards produced by aggressive shaking out of your drink. Double straining is a practice that is deemed necessary by many professional bartenders, but I do think there are occasions where a pristine-looking cocktail is called for and unsightly fragments of ice floating casually on the surface of the drink have no part to play in that scenario.

MUDDLER

On occasion it's necessary to get physical with some ingredients and engage in a bit of a scuffle. Whether it's squashing raspberries into submission or ruffling the tips of some mint leaves, extracting flavour from fresh ingredients is sometimes done using a 'muddler'. As stupid a name as it might be, it does exactly as one might expect.

Muddlers are like small police batons and generally made of plastic or wood. If you have a rolling pin in your house, you have no need to buy a muddler (use the money for a nice bottle of bourbon or gin instead) as the bakers' most prized tool will do the job just fine. Note: a muddler is a poor substitute for a rolling pin when flattening pastry.

CITRUS JUICER

As I have already mentioned, citrus presses are a useful component of your home cocktail cabinet but are

17

EQUIPMENT & ESSENTIALS

by no means essential. Having said that, lemons and limes are not getting any cheaper, so it's wise to extract every last drop of juice you possibly can from them.

A lever-style press (referred to by many as a Mexican elbow) is your best bet, and these contraptions do a nice job of liberating the oil from the skin of the citrus fruit too. A standard kitchen citrus reamer will work ok too.

KNIVES AND PEELERS

If you don't have a knife and vegetable peeler in your kitchen drawer already, it raises serious concerns about your commitment to freshly prepared food and drink! A small vegetable knife (or one of the razor-sharp serrated 'tomato' knives) fits the bill for chopping most fruits, and I opt for one of the 'Y' shaped vegetable peelers for stripping healthy lengths of citrus peels.

ICE PICK

Not the kind you go mountaineering with, but the kind of hand-held pick with one or three spikes on the end that is used to chip away at blocks of ice. This is one tool that can't be substituted easily with another kitchen implement so it's worth investing in one if you're planning on freezing big chunks of ice (which you should be doing).

GLASSWARE

Your favourite cocktail bar may stock a whole range of glassware finely tuned to meet the needs of different drinks, but truth be told 90% of cocktails can be served in one of three glasses: coupe, highball and old fashioned (also known as rocks).

Settle on a sensible-sized coupe that can handle both a tiny Martini or a shaken higher volume drink, such as a White Lady. The 150-ml/ 5-oz size is usually about right – it won't look like a half-full bucket when serving a Martini and it won't be full to the brim when mixing a Cosmopolitan.

Your highball and old fashioned will usually be around the same volume, only one will be taller and more narrow and the other more squat, heavier and wider. Think about which drinks you like to make the most and consider which size will suit them.

Of course you don't need to limit yourself to only these three glasses. In my time I have been known to quite contentedly consume cocktails from tea cups, egg cups or mixed directly back into the bottle. If the drink tastes good, it tastes good – most often the serviceware is there only to improve the experience and enhance the environment. If that environment is a camping trip, then why not drink a Manhattan from an enamel camping mug – anything else would be absurd!

For chilled cocktails that are served 'straight up' (ie no ice), the glasses should always be chilled before use. Serving a cold cocktail in a room-temperature glass is like serving a Sunday roast on a cold plate – the hot food cools down a lot quicker, just as a chilled drink will warm up a lot quicker.

I personally like to use glasses chilled in the refrigerator for most drinks. These glasses will be at around 1°C, which is an acceptable level above the common temperature range of most drinks (0°C to -5°C). Glasses from the freezer work too (and look cool!), but that freezing cold temperature can be a bit alarming to the lips on the first sip.

You can also chill glasses on the fly by adding a few lumps of ice and some water, then quickly stirring for a minute or so, emptying and pouring in the prepared cocktail.

Taking the time to ensure the glass is at the correct temperature is a simple step that makes a big difference. As with most things in the kitchen or bar, preparation is key.

COUPE

Martini

Rob Roy

Margarita

HIGHBALL

Mojito

Bloody Mary

Singapore Sling

OLD FASHIONED

Negroni

Sazerac

Mai Tai

Whisky Sour

KITCHEN INGREDIENTS

Unless you're content drinking cocktails made entirely from booze (which can be nice sometimes!), you will need a basic catalogue of kitchen ingredients. Now, there's a good chance you're holding stock of this stuff already, but it's worth taking the time to check before embarking upon an evening's cocktail making. Not all of the ingredients listed here are necessary for the cocktails featured in this kit, but should you wish to expand your repertoire further (and you really should), they will come in handy.

DRY INGREDIENTS

SUGAR - caster/superfine sugar is a staple product that can easily be converted into sugar syrups for cocktails, or used as a base for flavoured syrups. You may wish to experiment with darker sugars too, such as Demerara and muscovado – these work particularly well in cocktails that call for aged rum.

SALT - not an obvious cocktail ingredient, but salt performs a similar role in mixed drinks as it does in food: elevating flavour and softening bitterness, sweetness and acidity. Cocktails rarely taste salty, but a small pinch of salt will improve most drinks – you'll see I use it in the Lime Rickey and Piña Colada

recipes. Keep table salt for making syrups and infusions, and flaked sea salt for rimming glassware (as in a Margarita) and garnishing.

HONEY - A great modifier that can be used in place of sugar syrup in almost any cocktail, assuming you like the flavour of honey of course. Honey plays especially well with grain-based spirits like gin, vodka and whisky.

MAPLE SYRUP - Similarly to honey, maple syrup adds a buttery, candied note to mixed drinks, and it works rather well with American whiskey.

AGAVE NECTAR - Disproven as a health food it might be – but you're not drinking Margaritas because they're healthy, right? – agave nectar certainly has a strong affinity with agave spirits (Tequila, mescal) as well as cachaca and agricole rums.

HERBS

Fresh herbs can be used as visually attractive and aromatically pleasing garnishes as well as components of

the cocktail itself. Fresh herbs can be tricky to store however. Too much moisture can make the leaves go slimy and too little moisture makes them dry out, while excessive light turns them yellow.

Store soft herbs like mint, basil and coriander/cilantro in the fridge, but arrange them like a bunch of flowers in a glass jar with water in the bottom.

Woody herbs, like rosemary, thyme and sage, should also be refrigerated, but last longer when wrapped in damp kitchen towel and placed in a sealable container.

CITRUS

Citrus fruits store reasonably well and provide theatrical and aromatic effect when freshly squeezed into a drink. Lime is generally the sourest of the family and can be as sour as 1.8 pH. Lime is comprised of both citric and ascorbic acid, whereas lemon is almost entirely citric acid and around 2.3 pH. Orange and grapefruit have a similar pH to one another of around 3.7 (oranges have more sugar in them, so taste less sour).

EGGS

The use of eggs, egg yolks and egg whites in cocktails has a long history. Many old-fashioned drinks like flips, possets and syllabubs require a whole egg for both a flavour and textural addition to a drink. Lots of cocktails that emerged from the golden era of mixed drinks (1860–1930) also call for egg white in the drink.

SODAS

It may sound simple, but keeping a good stock of sodas can be a bit of a challenge as they tend to lose their fizz quite quickly. This is something that you can let slide when it's just a glass of fizz you're after, but a G&T without the bubbles is a sorry affair, just as a Mojito without that lick of spritz can also feel a bit flat.

Soda water, tonic water, ginger beer and Coca-Cola make up the four pillars of your carbonated world.

ICE

The simplest mistake when setting up a home bar is not enough ice. As a rule, you're going to need about twice as much ice as you think you will. Cocktails get through lots of ice and too little ice in the preparation or service of a drink will always result in an inferior looking and tasting drink.

Try to reserve a drawer in your freezer purely for ice, so you can store ice cubes and larger lengths, even blocks of ice that can be chipped away at if the feeling takes you.

It's cubed ice that will be the bread and butter of your drink-making regime however, so invest in some large ice-cube trays and get used to freezing, dumping and refilling them when you have a spare moment.

You may wish to purchase a hand-operated ice-crusher – these items are inexpensive and produce good-quality ice nuggets that can be used for a variety of (usually) rum-based cocktails. A dish towel and a mallet can work

as a last resort, but it can be tricky to achieve a consistent quality with this method. Blenders cannot be used to make crushed ice – they make snow.

The shape and size of the ice used makes little difference to the final temperature and dilution of a drink. Crushed, cubed and even big rocks of hand-cracked ice of the same weight all eventually achieve about the same levels of dilution and temperature. Only the time this takes changes because the surface areas of the different ice types vary. Stirring with crushed ice might take a Martini down to -5°C in ten seconds, but stirring the same Martini with the same weight of hand-cracked ice can take over two minutes to achieve the same levels of temperature and dilution.

The golden rule, no matter what type of ice you use, is to always take it straight from the freezer. Ice from the freezer is colder, of course, but crucially it is not 'wet' (partially melted) and therefore not going to unnecessarily dilute your drink.

THE SCIENCE OF FLAVOUR

◆

There's a lot going on when you take a sip of that Martini. Tongue, mouth, nose, eyes and even ears work in harmony to glean every ounce of relevant information about the drink you're sipping. In fact, flavour is amongst the most complex perceptions created by our brains. Let us first see a description of how flavour is produced by flavour psychologist Jean Anthelme Brillat-Savarin in 1825:

> *Man's apparatus of the sense of taste has been brought to a state of rare perfection; and, to convince ourselves thoroughly, let us watch it at work.*
>
> *As soon as an edible body has been put into the mouth, it is seized upon, gases, moisture, and all, without possibility of retreat.*
>
> *Lips stop whatever might try to escape; the teeth bite and break it;*

> *saliva drenches it: the tongue mashes and churns it; a breathlike sucking pushes it toward the gullet; the tongue lifts up to make it slide and slip; the sense of smell appreciates it as it passes the nasal channel, and it is pulled down into the stomach... without... a single atom or drop or particle having been missed by the powers of appreciation of the taste sense.*

Brillat-Savarin, *Physiologie du Goût* (The Physiology of Taste), 1825

It is fairly common knowledge that as much as 80% of flavour is recognised as a result of the nose, rather than the mouth. This is mostly true, though it's difficult to quantify exactly how much work the nose does in comparison to all the multi-sensory (or multimodal) inputs that the brain utilises. The brain's ability to combine taste, touch and smell into a unified flavour image is called synesthesia.

SMELL

Much of this 'flavour-mapping' work is conducted through retro-nasal smell, that is 'backward' smell, through the back of the nose.

As we gargle, masticate, swill and swallow, tiny aromatic molecules, only visible on an atomic level, are exhaled up through the throat and out of the nose. As they pass through the nasal passage, they come into contact with the olfactory epithelium – this nasal tissue is the nose's direct hardline to the brain. It sends minute signals to the olfactory bulb, which converts signals into a smell image, the main component of flavour. Contrary to whatever bad publicity you may have heard about the human sense of smell, it is truly an incredible thing – better, in fact, than even the most advanced molecule-detecting equipment that our brains have been able to devise.

TASTE

Taste and the palate also play an important role in flavour perception. Taste begins with the taste buds – a collection of sensory cells, each with fine hairs that respond to stimuli. Taste buds are located within the tiny visible folds on the surface of the tongue, known as papillae. The different receptors in taste cells detect five primary tastes: salt, sweet, sour, bitter and umami (a savoury-like taste which is particularly common in tomatoes, soy and Parmesan cheese).

These tastes are detected all over the tongue, though some areas have higher concentrations of specific receptors. Signals are sent to the brain for processing, along with other sensory input.

The tongue and mouth also conduct the important role of detecting mouth-feel. Although more relevant to eating than drinking, mouth-feel can have a profound effect on our appreciation of cocktails. Mouth-feel is not a wholly understood science, but it is known to include such sensory submodalities as touch, pressure, temperature and pain. Each of these affects the image of flavour in different ways. Ever noticed how flat cola tastes different to fizzy cola? That'll be the pain receptors in your mouth altering the flavour image when triggered by the tickling of CO_2 gas in the bubbles of your coke.

VISION

In the most basic form, our eyes tell us whether something will fit into our mouths, and whether or not it's likely to hurt us. But going deeper, the way that a drink looks plays a huge part in how we determine its flavour. I'm not just talking about pretty garnishes (although they do help), but fundamental things such as colour, size, glassware and temperature indication (frosted, steam).

My favourite experiment, which I have conducted on several occasions, is feeding someone blue tomato juice (made by agar clarification and blue food colouring). Even though the taste and aroma have not been altered at all, most subjects fail to recognise the drink as tomato juice, simply because the colour has no relevance to the fruit. Once a lady that I gave blue tomato juice to told me that it tasted like laundry fluid – clearly she was heavily influenced by the bright blue colour.

SOUND

Even sound has an important part to play in the discovery of flavour. The French playwright Molière described the sound of wine as 'glouglou':

How sweet from you
My bottle true;
How sweet from you
Your little glouglou

Act 1, Scene 5, *The Doctor in Spite of Himself*, 1666

And it is true that red wine has an entirely unique sound over other liquids. The glouglou sound of wine as we swallow is the muscle activity in our throats processing red wine's unique texture.

OTHER FACTORS

There is a huge variety of other factors that are thought to contribute towards the 'flavour map' of a drink - even our sense of well-being, comfort and the environment around us affect flavour. Hot soup is better when you're cold and a chilled glass of Sauvignon Blanc tastes better when you're hot. Likewise, continental beers never taste as good as when sipped on a hot sandy beach in their country of origin. A dish from childhood, such as your mother's shepherds pie, will always taste better (or worse) than any other, since it evokes a sense of nostalgia.

The human appreciation of flavour is a marvellous thing, and something that should be exercised, enjoyed and tested wherever possible. The complex neural pathways that process the data input from our senses all converge in a part of the brain called the primate neocortex. Here we experience a conscious flavour perception, something that is tangible within our minds. And perhaps the smartest trick of all is that of the brain reflecting the data back down to the tongue and fooling us into thinking the whole experience took place in our mouth!

COCKTAIL TASTE SCIENCE

Looking at the last 200 years of cocktail evolution, we have seen some clues as to why we have landed upon such an eclectic selection of drinks. Many of the advances in cocktail preparation give key indicators as to why we prefer to enjoy drinks one way more than another, and it's these drinks coupled with the complexities of the human perception of flavour that have laid the path for cocktail creators over the years.

We can now go a step further, into the component tastes of a cocktail, and see both how they affect our sense of perception and how they affect each other in the context of a cocktail. Primary taste sensations of saltiness or sweetness are well known to us, but what is not as fully understood is the complex relationships that these tastes have with each other and how they play a role in balancing drinks.

SUGAR Sugar is pure energy. As humans we love the stuff – hell, you can add sugar to almost anything and we'll probably enjoy it more. There is a primal desire for sugar programmed into every one of us right from birth.

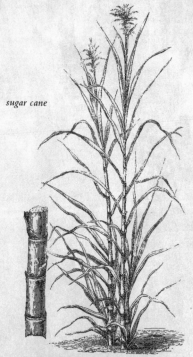

sugar cane

Sugar does have the effect of slightly reducing the perception of alcohol in a drink. Exactly why this is the case is not clear, though it might be partly due to sugar reducing the volatility of the alcohol (how readily it will evaporate). It could also be a result of the brain's 'reward' system, wherein the effect of the alcohol is lessened as a result of the positive sweet trigger. Our reward system recognises the calories present in the sugar and chooses to ignore the negative chemesthesis effects (see page 38) of the alcohol. Liqueurs are the perfect case in point. Think about how a 40% ABV liqueur slips down a lot easier than 40% straight vodka.

Tests have shown that sugar suppresses the intensity of bitter, acidic and salty flavours, too. But it does more than that: it actually makes those other tastes more pleasurable than if they were stand-alone – the satisfaction of a bitter-sweet glass of ale, the refreshing acid sting of a kiwi fruit, the indulgence of salted caramel.

BITTERNESS Bitterness is by far the most complicated of the taste senses. It is thought that the tongue detects over 100 different types of bitterness (salt is just salt), and the molecules that have a bitter taste come in various different shapes and sizes.

Unlike sugar, we are programmed with an aversion to bitterness. It's thought that this is as a result of most bitter substances being poisonous in big enough quantities. (The flip side of this is that in smaller quantities bitter ingredients are often medicinal – think of the anaesthetic effect of chewing on a clove, the antimalarial properties of quinine and the stomach-settling qualities of holly bush tea. It's for this reason that certain primate species have been observed chewing on bitter plant roots and tree bark when they are feeling unwell.)

Remember your first cup of black coffee? Or your first lager? Chances are that it didn't go down all that well and that's because Mother

Nature wants you to hate bitterness! Bitterness on its own is not nice, and it would require a huge amount of sensory training to convince your brain otherwise.

But we're not going to give in that easily! The problem for Mother Nature lies in the fact that bitterness has a strange drying effect on the tongue that makes you want to refresh your palate. When we drink something intensely bitter, it's almost like an instant thirst inducer, meaning that another sip is required. And another. So when bitterness is accompanied by aromatics and sweetness (and salt – see right), it can become incredibly addictive! The best example of this is the classic gin and tonic – surely one of the greatest refreshments the world has known.

Adding bitters to mixed drinks helps us to engineer a more interesting and complex cocktail by fusing together intense bitterness with other taste and aromatic stimuli.

ACIDITY When we eat or drink something intensely sour, we screw our faces up and wince in the wake of it. Intense sourness is experienced negatively, since its consumption generally has no nutritional benefits – why waste energy eating it?

On the plus side, however, acidity does an excellent job of balancing other taste sensations. If you have ever eaten 'miracle fruit' (an African berry that when consumed temporarily blocks certain taste receptors, resulting in everything tasting sweet), you will have noticed how bland a world it is when there is no acidity to balance sweetness. Without sourness, ripe fruit is simply sweet; even the accompanying aromatics in a fresh peach fail to deliver that heady feeling of gustatory perfection, since there is no acid either to balance the sweetness or to grip the palate.

In cocktails we often use sourness, balanced with sweetness, to emulate the taste of ripe fruit. Limes and lemons are mostly used, since they

have a relatively neutral flavour profile dominated almost entirely by their sourness. For more on acids, see page 25.

SALT According to Hervé This's 2006 book, *Molecular Gastronomy*:

> '[Salts] selectively suppress bitterness (and probably other disagreeable tastes as well) while intensifying agreeable tastes.'

In my experience, a small addition of salt (0.1–0.3%) almost always improves the taste of a cocktail, cordial, liqueur or syrup. The one major exception being if the product is already noticeably salty – through the use of a salty ingredient, perhaps. It is curious, then, that it is such an under-utilised ingredient in cocktails. A great example of where it is used is in the Gin Rickey. This drink is basically a Gin Fizz, or Tom Collins, but with lime juice substituted for lemon juice. Yet in some cultures, most notably India, the sugar is omitted and a small amount of salt is used in its place. What, on paper, would appear be a very sour drink actually becomes softer and really very tasty. Salt is a much more common beverage ingredient in hot climates, since in the right quantities it is thought to aid in maintaining adequate hydration.

Salt lowers perception of sourness significantly, but only slightly affects the intensity of bitter or sweet things.

UMAMI The discovery of the fifth taste, umami, seems like a new thing, but it was actually over 100 years ago, in 1908, that Kikunae Ikeda at the Tokyo Imperial University established its existence. Not salty, sweet, sour or bitter, umami produces a strange sensation that can best be described as savoury. Umami is not a taste that crops up all that often in cocktails. Sure, the tomato juice family of drinks – Bloody Mary, Red Snapper et al. – have their fair share of savoury kick, but it pretty much ends there. Given the strong savoury connotations of umami (if you've never tried it, miso soup or just pure monosodium glutamate (MSG) are a safe bet as long as you can ignore the saltiness of the soup), it's not all that surprising that bartenders use very little, since one of the main functions of a cocktail is to whet the appetite, not suppress it.

ALCOHOL Almost all spirits have some flavour, even the vodkas. This may come from residual fusel oils or higher alcohols remaining from the distillation process, or traces of the product that the spirit is made from. In the case of vodka, this might be a slight cereal note, or a buttery potato flavour.

Pure ethanol (alcohol) is almost completely flavourless. However, when mixed with water at certain specific concentrations, it does have a slightly bitter-sweet taste. In addition to this, ethanol and acetone (a flavourful ketone) both have a dehydrating effect on the palate, which in turn gives a sense of astringency. Chemesthesis is a term meaning the feel or sensibility of a chemical – ethanol in this case – on the skin, taste buds, mucous membranes, throat and stomach. Alcohol plays havoc with certain nerve channels and the result is the perception of burning. It just so happens that the same nerves triggered by alcohol are the ones triggered by capsaicin (the stuff that makes chillies hot). While pain isn't a taste per se, it does have a knock-on effect on our perception of tastes and aromas.

THE SCIENCE OF FLAVOUR

TEN BOTTLES

A ll ingredients are equal, but some are more equal than others. While it's true that some cocktails require highly specific brands or styles, most of the time the exact product that you choose to use won't be of critical importance. It's a common understanding that a cocktail is only as strong as its weakest link, but in reality not all links in the chain are of equal size.

If you're making a Martini, the gin is an important consideration as it is at the forefront of the flavour profile, so a little more care in selection is required. In a cocktail such as the Negroni, where the gin battles against far more powerful flavours than that of the dry vermouth in the Martini, there is clearly less need to be fastidious about the brand of gin. In fact unless you're using a gin with wildly extreme botanicals, or one that tastes bad, in all likelihood your Negroni will taste good made with most brands of gin.

I liken it (like a lot of things) to cooking. If you're making spaghetti alla bolognese, the exact cut of minced/ground beef is not as important as the tomatoes, cooking time, quality of the pasta etc. If you're frying a steak, however, the cut of beef becomes a very important factor. Which is more important in a Bloody Mary – the brand of vodka or the quality of the tomato juice?

What I'm trying to say here is that in most cases it's ok to select a single brand from each of the main spirit categories (vodka, gin, rum, tequila, whisky, cognac) and stick with it for the majority of your cocktail making. This practice will save you a lot of space and expense and ensure that your spirit cupboard doesn't contain a bunch of dusty neglected bottles.

My main piece of advice is that you make sure you pick one that is versatile, of a premium quality and pleasing to drink neat. For most drinks a generic spirit from the given category will do, but in some instances certain cocktails call for quite specific spirits (you just can't put a Navy rum in a mojito, for example), so I will do my best to point out any drinks where I believe that a specific style, age or brand of liquor is required.

GIN

More classic cocktails have gin as their base than any other spirit. Indeed, if you were a bartender practising your trade in the 1920s, the vast majority of the drinks you would be asked for would contain gin. For me, gin is all about juniper, so opt

for a classic style such as Beefeater or Tanqueray. There are, of course, many newer brands that will also fit the bill.

RUM

A spirit derived from sugar cane, rum is a key component to many classic punch drinks, most notably those from Cuba and drinks that fall under the category of tiki.

It's difficult to buy a one-size-fits-all bottle of rum, as some drinks call for lighter styles (un-aged or lightly aged) typical of the Spanish-speaking islands and others for much heavier styles that you might find in Jamaica or Guyana. A good compromise is a light Barbados or St. Lucia rum, such as Doorly's or Chairman's Reserve.

SCOTCH

A decent blended scotch is what we're after here and it needn't break the bank. Avoid anything too smoky as this may imbalance the cocktail, and look for fruit and malt characteristics. Johnnie Walker Gold Label Reserve, Dewars 12 or Chivas Regal 12 will all do the job fine.

BOURBON

American whiskey is a staple ingredient of many a pre-Prohibition cocktail. Drinks of that era also used rye whiskey as a base, which takes on a slightly spicier flavour when compared to the slick sweetness of bourbon's higher corn content. A good compromise is Woodford Reserve or Bulleit, both of them bourbons that contain a healthy measure of rye in the mash bills.

COGNAC

French brandy was the original mixing spirit in the mid-19th century, and it remains a fantastically versatile cocktail ingredient (and one that is unrecognised as a cocktail base). A good VSOP from any of the major Cognac houses will work perfectly well here, though if you want my recommendation I would suggest looking at Pierre Ferrand.

TEQUILA

The golden rule when buying tequila is only buy a bottle that says 100% agave on the label. If it doesn't say this, it means the spirit contains some corn- or wheat-based distillate, which serves to boost the alcohol content and dilute the natural vegetal flavours of the plant upon which the drink should be based. Aged tequila can taste quite different to the unaged stuff, so to cover all bases I suggest using a reposed ('rested') tequila which will have been aged for between 2 and 12 months.

VODKA

Let's not sugarcoat it – nine times out of ten it's difficult to discern the difference in a vodka once it's been mixed into a cocktail. That one time however, such as when you mix a Vodka Martini or a Vesper, will demand a decent liquid so it's worth buying something you'd be happy to sip on. My recommendation is for a rye vodka like Belvedere or Vestal, or a potato vodka like Chase.

TRIPLE SEC

Triple sec (meaning extra dry in French) is similar to curaçao which has its origins in the Dutch island of the same name. Both are orange liqueurs made from the peels of bitter oranges, but curaçao tends to be sweeter. I would recommend a triple sec such as Cointreau and the recipes I provide are based on a spirit of that sweetness.

VERMOUTH

If you're looking for a one-bottle solution to vermouth, I suggest plumping for a bianco style, which is light in colour but still rather sweet. If your budget can stretch to two bottles, get one extra-dry (French style) and one sweet (a.k.a rosso, Italian style).

Always store your vermouth in the fridge and aim to finish the bottle within 30 days (tip: mix it with soda and ice for a delicious alternative to a white wine spritzer).

AMARI

Bitter aperitivo like Campari or Aperol are fantastic ingredients to keep around because they make delicious long cocktails like the Americano, as well as being the chief component of the legendary Negroni cocktail.

Ten is a nice round number, and with the bottles listed on the previous pages you'll do just fine. But if you will allow me, here are another three bottles that will truly elevate your craft. If the last ten bottles were the meat and vegetables of your cocktail-making regime, these next three are the condiments and sauces.

ABSINTHE

Contrary to what you might have heard (or perhaps experienced), absinthe is not the hallucination-inducing poison that it is sometimes portrayed as. It is typically quite high in alcohol (this is to stop the liquid from looking cloudy as it contains oils that fall out of solution in low-

alcohol conditions), but it is not designed to be consumed this way.

Absinthe is best imbibed with plenty of ice-cold water, or as an ingredient in such classic cocktails as Sazerac and Corpse Reviver No. 2. The best brands are those produced by Jade, as well as Butterfly and La Clandestine.

MARASCHINO

This cherry-flavoured liqueur is arguably just as important as triple sec in the field of cocktail modification. It came into popularity around the same time as its orange counterpart too. Maraschino has miraculous mixing powers, and the ability to pull a poor-tasting drink out of a nose dive just from a splash. Luxardo is the go-to brand here.

DRY AMONTILLADO SHERRY

Yes, I am a bit of a sherry fiend, but it's also my belief that a small drop of sherry will have the effect of improving virtually any cocktail it comes into contact with. It often works well in place of vermouth too, and there are great classic cocktails such as the Sherry Cobbler that rely on sherry as the base ingredient.

MAKING A DRINK

It might seem like a no-brainer to stress the importance of how you shake, stir and use ice. But it's easy to overlook the complexity of these techniques and in doing so, overlook some crucial variables that can be manipulated to your advantage. Both the temperature and the degree of dilution of a cocktail are key contributors to the enjoyment of the cocktail, so insuring they are managed correctly is a hugely important part of bar craft.

The common belief is that colder drinks taste better. As temperature lowers, the drink becomes more viscous, texture becomes thicker and more pleasant. Alcohol evaporation is suppressed so that the initial hit of liquor feels softer and increases gently as the drink warms on the tongue. Low temperature also provides a greater feeling of refreshment and cleansing to the palate. Very cold drinks also have less aroma.

Vapour pressure is a term that describes how readily a liquid vaporises, and it's the liquid's vapour that we smell when we stick our noses into a glass of wine. Vapour pressure lowers as temperature lowers, meaning that colder drinks have less aroma. This has an interesting effect when we come to drink a cocktail, as when the liquid quickly heats up in your mouth it begins to pump increasingly intense waves of aroma down your throat and back out through your nose as you breathe.

Good chilling goes hand in hand with ice meltage. Many bartenders have created elaborate routines to limit dilution, but the truth is that a bit of dilution in a drink can actually be a positive thing. But when does not enough dilution become too much? Looking at different bottles of gin, you can see from the wide variety of bottle strengths that producers are careful to package the product at exactly the right ABV to best show off the flavour. The same is true for cocktails – the ABV of a finished drink will affect both the taste of the drink and the aroma, where a little extra water can persuade a greater number of aromatic molecules to escape the glass (which is why water is often added to whisky).

Most of the time dilution is a subjective science, but I have found that sometimes the amount of water in a cocktail is of critical importance and can easily ruin a drink when insufficient care is taken. The key is understanding how and why chilling and dilution occur, then adjusting our techniques to achieve the results we're after – just as a chef adjusts cooking time to meet the needs of each individual dish.

SHAKING

Shaking a cocktail chills it quickly. This is in part because the agitation of the ice and liquid speeds up the process of equilibrium, but also because the ice cracks and breaks, increasing its surface area. Shaking a drink for more than ten seconds will have very little further affect on temperature or dilution. This is because as the cocktail approaches its freezing point, its temperature plateaus. At this point the level of dilution will also plateau, since the ice is only required to stabilise the temperature of the drink (against the warm air outside of the shaker), rather than chill it.

Shaken drinks are also 'aerated' to a degree – the action of whipping up the cocktail with ice causes air bubbles to become trapped in the liquid for a time. We are able to detect these tiny bubbles on the palate, and they can profoundly affect the tactile experience of the

cocktail and the way in which flavour is perceived.

The vibrant Japanese bar scene has contributed a number of great things to western bartending over the past few years, the most useful of all being the wide selection of quality barware and tools. Another significant influence that has come out of Japan has made a lot of western bartenders reconsider the way in which they shake. When I first heard about the 'Japanese hard shake' I assumed it was a way of shaking a drink hard (which makes sense), but if anything it should refer to how hard it is to master.

The aim is to bounce the ice off every surface of the shaker by moving the shaker in a highly specific pattern. It looks a lot like a dance step, but with a cocktail shaker. The intended result is a drink that, quite simply, feels better. The pioneer of the technique, Uyeda San of Tender Bar in Tokyo, is adamant that the drink is better in every way, but in tests

I have discovered that the pattern in which you shake (as long as it's not excessively slow) makes no difference to the temperature or dilution of the cocktail – once again science wins over. That leaves only the element of aeration. Sadly, measuring aeration and viscosity is much harder to do and requires in-depth qualitative testing to be able to truly determine whether the hard shake really does make a better drink.

Be sure to use plenty of ice in the shaker – fill it two-thirds full for a single drink and add extra ice if you're shaking a lot of liquid. Clip the lid or tin on to the shaker and give it a fast and hard shake for five to ten seconds.

STIRRING

A strong drink can be chilled to -3°C in under ten seconds by shaking it with cubed ice, but to achieve the same result by stirring with cubed ice will take over 30 seconds. This is because a stir is, in a sense, a very slow shake. You can be forgiven for assuming that a stirred drink has more dilution because it takes longer, but the physics are the same whether the drink is shaken or stirred - if a cocktail is stirred for long enough, it will reach almost exactly the same temperature and dilution as if it were shaken. I say almost, because the longer exposure to the warm air surrounding the beaker will create some extra dilution in the drink.

The most important thing to understand about stirring is that it takes rather a long time – more than a minute in many cases if you're aiming for really low temperatures. Remember that chilling and dilution plateau in the same way as shaking – after around 120 seconds (depending on the size of the ice) the drink won't get much colder and it won't get much more diluted.

You can tell if a cocktail is being stirred well because it's an almost silent process. Ice should not be 'clinking' around (this creates bubbles and chips of ice) but spinning fluidly around the circumference of the beaker or tin. As with shaking, plenty of ice is needed and the level of liquid in the beaker/tin should fall well under the level of ice. Generally speaking, a one-minute stir should do the trick, but it's fine to go up to two minutes (if you can wait that long).

BUILDING

There are a lot of cocktails that are quite delicious when simply built over ice in the glass. Besides requiring less equipment and making less mess, there is something rather satisfying about enjoying a drink from the glass that you mix it in. Approach building in the same way as you would approach a stirred drink.

BLENDED

Blenders are becoming a less common sight in modern cocktail bars, but there are still some classic cocktails that can only be created in a blender and other drinks (the Ramos Gin Fizz, for example) that can benefit from being blended.

In most instances a blended drink will call for the same weight or volume of ice as the volume of liquid ingredients. Blended drinks must be served immediately as they are prone to 'splitting', which is where the slushy ice floats on top of the liquid drink.

TEN TIPS FOR ACHIEVING PERFECTION

◆

There are countless tips and tricks that can elevate your cocktail-making game, whether it's to help you make even better tasting drinks or to aid in keeping things clean, tidy and efficient. I don't claim to know them all, but after nearly twenty years working behind bars I do know a few.

Make your own sugar syrup. Sugar syrup (or gomme) can be made in a pan on the stove. Simply mix two parts sugar with one part water and heat until the liquid becomes clear. Let the mixture cool and add a splash of vodka (this slows down the rate of spoilage) – roughly equivalent to 10% of the total weight of the syrup. Store in the fridge for up to three months.

Pre-squeeze fruit juices. Squeezing lemons and limes is one of the messiest parts of constructing a drink so it's far better to do it in advance if you can. Fresh citrus will start to taste a bit nasty after 24–48 hours, but at under 12 hours old it tastes perfectly fine. Store in the fridge.

Careful with sweet stuff. When mixing with syrups or sweet condiments, don't add them to the glass or shaker first as they have a tendency to stick to the glass or shaker as they chill and become difficult to remove.

Add cheaper ingredients first. This helps to avoid sickening scenarios such as having to pour your XO Cognac down the sink because you accidentally reached for crème de menthe instead of triple sec when making a Sidecar.

Clean as you go. A quick rinse of a shaker or glass will speed things up when you come to making your next drink or next round of drinks.

Pre-mix liquids. For ingredients that won't spoil (syrups or anything with an alcohol content), you can save yourself a lot of time and improve consistency by pre-mixing them. In the case of a Negroni, for example, why not mix equal parts of Campari, gin and vermouth in a clean bottle and store in the fridge, ready for stirring over ice?

Invest in spare equipment. While it's always sensible to clean as you go, having a stock of spare shakers, mixing beakers and jiggers comes in handy when you need to make a lot of different drinks all at once. Stack them up where possible to save space.

Give yourself enough space. One of the gravest errors of home bartending is expecting to produce dozens of drinks on a worktop the size of a postage stamp. You need space and you need a sink to wash up in. Arrange your equipment, bottles, towels and a cloth carefully and try to keep these items in their designated areas.

Think about round building. Round building is more relevant to professional bartending, but it can come in handy in the home too. Try to get into the practice of visualising every ingredient you need to make a round of drinks and imagine only touching each bottle once. For example, by pouring all of the lemon juice you need for a given round all in one go, you save time later by not needing to return to it.

Stick to the recipe. I've said it already, but it bears repeating. Always stick to the correct ratios and you will not go wrong. A cocktail is nothing more than a mathematical formula, but if you change things the formula gets broken.

GLOSSARY

ABV Alcohol by volume.

Acetone A flavourful ketone.

Agave Thick fibrous plant, the heart (or piña) of which is cooked and used to make tequila.

Atomize To spritz or spray aroma, usually directed at glassware or the surface of a drink.

Bar spoon A long-handled, weighted spoon, used for stirring drinks and floating and layering ingredients.

Batch The process of pre-mixing liquids together and storing them for later use.

Boston A cocktail shaker comprised of a large metal tin and a glass that should fit snugly inside the tin.

Botanical Fruit, herb, flower or spice used to flavour gin during distillation process.

Chemesthesis The irritation or burn of a chemical (including alcohol) on the palate or skin.

Citric acid Acid found in lemons and other citrus fruit.

Citrus juicer (or citrus press) Useful for extracting every last drop of juice.

Coupe Stemmed glass (one of the three main styles of glassware).

Distillation Process of separating alcohol and/or other volatile compounds from a mixture, based on their boiling points. Controlled through heat and air pressure. Most commonly used to extract ethanol from an ethanol–water mixture.

Dry shake The act of shaking a cocktail that contains egg white twice – once with ice and once without – in order to create a foamy head on the drink.

Fusel oils Generic term describing heavy (high boiling-point) alcohols produced during fermentation that add characterful, heavy flavours to distillations.

Gomme Sugar syrup used to sweeten drinks containing an emulsifier such as gum arabic.

Hawthorn strainer Perforated metal plate with a coil of wire running around the edge.

Highball Tall, narrow glass (one of the three main styles of glassware).

Jigger A vital piece of the cocktail-maker's kit as it allows you to meaure ingredients accurately.

Julep strainer Can be used for straining stirred cocktails.

Ketone Organic, often flavour-providing compound.

Mexican elbow Lever-style citrus press.

Mixing beaker Large, open-topped vessel for stirring drinks.

Muddler Used to gently crush ingredients to extract juice and flavour.

Neutral spirit Spirit distilled above 96% ABV and made from cereal, potato, grape, molasses or any other sugar or starch source. Can be denoted as grain, which infers that cereal is the base product.

Old fashioned Squat, heavy glass (one of the three main styles of glassware).

Olfactory epithelium Smell pad located between the eyes

and the first stage of the brain, for detecting aroma.

Orthonasal (smell) Aroma carried through the front of the nose up to the olfactory epithelium.

Osmotic pressure Force required for a liquid to break through a semipermeable membrane. In the case of fruit, it is the force required for a liquid to leach out through the skin or membrane of the fruit.

Papillae Visible collection of taste buds on the tongue.

Pot still Traditional kettle-style still.

Retronasal (smell) Aroma carried through the back of the mouth and into the nasal passage.

Rocks Another name for an old fashioned glass.

Shaker Available in different styles, and used – unsurprisingly – for mixing and shaking cocktails.

Sour A family of cocktails that typically comprises spirit, citrus juice, sugar and egg white.

Straight up A cocktail served without ice, generally in a martini glass or coupe.

Sugar syrup A simple syrup used to sweeten drinks with a 2:1 ratio of sugar to water. To make about 1 litre/1 quart sugar syrup, gently heat 660 g/23 oz. caster/granulated sugar (you can also use soft brown/muscovado sugar) with 300 ml/10 oz. water and 30 g/1 oz. vodka in a saucepan. Once all the sugar has dissolved, bottle it and pop it in the fridge for up to 6 months.

Synaesthesia Concept of the brain combining sensory input to create a 'flavour image'.

Umami The fifth taste (alongside salty, sweet, sour and bitter), umami is best described as savoury.

Vapour pressure A term to describe how quickly a liquid vaporises.

Drinks photography:

Addie Chinn pages 2, 22, 28, 35, 42, 43, 64, all cocktail recipe cards;
Gavin Kingcome pages 11, 14-18, 27, 39, 40, 50-57;
William Lingwood pages 8, 12.

Illustrations and other photography:

Page 21, back cover Selina Snow; page 23 Keith Bishop/iStock; page 24 Belloott/iStock; page 25 nicoolay/iStock; page 29 Granger Historical Picture Archive/Alamy; page 33 Nikola Nastasic/iStock; page 37 Sketch Master/Shutterstock.com; page 44a Ultima_Gaina/iStock; page 44b Todd Williamson/Getty Images; page 45a www.maisonferrand.com; page 45b Douglas Rial/iStock; page 46 www.vestalvodka.com; page 47l monticelllo/iStock; page 47c verbaska_studio/iStock; page 47r popovaphoto/iStock; page 48 Image by Benjamin Krick of Juniper Tar/San Antonio, Texas www.juniper-tar.com; page 49l www.luxardococktails.com; page 49r www.equiponavazos.com

EQUIPMENT & SUPPLIERS

UK

The Whisky Exchange
Renowned online retailer of
spirits. They specialise in whisky
but stock much more besides,
including a good range of
vintage spirits.
www.whiskyexchange.com

Master of Malt
Online retailer of spirits (not
only whisky), vermouth and
other cocktail ingredients.
www.masterofmalt.com

Drinkshop
General glassware and cocktail
equipment – absinthe fountains,
large selection of glassware and
basic equipment. Online.
www.thedrinkshop.com

House of Fraser
Good range of glassware and
cocktail equipment. Online and
stores across the UK.
www.houseoffraser.co.uk

Liberty
Good range of glassware and
cocktail equipment. Online and
London store.
www.libertylondon.com

Oliver Bonas
Good range of glassware and
cocktail equipment. Online and
over 30 stores around the UK.
www.oliverbonas.com

Fenwick
Good range of glassware and
cocktail equipment. Online and
over 10 stores in the UK.
www.fenwick.co.uk

John Lewis
Good range of glassware and
cocktail equipment. Online and
stores across the UK.
www.johnlewis.com

USA

Cocktail Kingdom
Purveyors of mid to high price
barware, and specialist in Japanese
equipment and glassware. Online
and New York store.
www.cocktailkingdom.com

Williams Sonoma
Good range of glassware and
cocktail equipment. Online and
stores across the US.
www.williams-sonoma.com

Pottery Barn
Good range of glassware and
cocktail equipment. Online and
stores across the US.
www.potterybarn.com

West Elm
Good range of glassware and
cocktail equipment. Online and
stores across the US.
www.westelm.com

Target
Good range of glassware and
cocktail equipment. Online
and stores across the US.
www.target.com

Crate & Barrel
Good range of glassware and
cocktail equipment. Online
and stores across the US.
www.crateandbarrel.com

Fishs Eddy
Good range of glassware and
cocktail equipment. Online
and New York store.
www.fishseddy.com

Neiman Marcus
Good range of glassware and
cocktail equipment. Online
and stores across the US.
www.neimanmarcus.com

IRELAND

Brown Thomas
Good range of glassware and
cocktail equipment. Online and
several stores across Ireland.
www.brownthomas.com

INDEX

ABOUT THE AUTHOR

Tristan Stephenson is an award-winning bar operator, bartender, barista, chef, some-time journalist and author of the bestselling *Curious Bartender* series of drinks books, all published by Ryland Peters & Small. He is the co-founder of London-based Fluid Movement, a globally renowned drinks consultancy firm, and half the brains behind the drinks programmes at some of the world's top drinking and eating destinations. In 2009 he was ranked 3rd in the UK Barista Championships. He was awarded UK bartender of the year in 2012 and in the same year was included in *London Evening Standard*'s 'Top 1000 most influential Londoners'.

Having started his career in the kitchens of various Cornish restaurants, Tristan joined Jamie Oliver's Fifteen restaurant in Cornwall in 2006 where he designed cocktails and ran bar operations. After co-founding Fluid Movement in 2009, Tristan opened two bars in London: Purl in 2010 and Worship Street Whistling Shop in 2011. Worship Street Whistling Shop was awarded *Time Out London*'s best new bar in 2011 and has been placed in the 'World's Fifty Best Bars' for three consecutive years. In 2014 Fluid Movement opened Surfside, a steak and lobster restaurant in Cornwall which was awarded the No. 1 Position in the *Sunday Times* 'Best alfresco dining spots in the UK 2015'. In 2016 Fluid Movement opened Black Rock, a breakthrough whisky bar which was awarded 2017 Best Specialist Bar in the UK by *Class* magazine. This was followed by the launch of Napoleon Hotel in east London, heralded as London's smallest grand hotel and containing two bars: Sack, a sherry bar inspired by the traditional tobaccos of Andalucia, and The Devil's Darling, a cocktail bar specialising in classic mixed drinks.

Tristan's first book, *The Curious Bartender: The Artistry & Alchemy of Creating the Perfect Cocktail*, was published in 2013 and shortlisted for the prestigious André Simon Award. His subsequent books are *The Curious Bartender: An Odyssey of Malt, Bourbon & Rye Whiskies* (2014), *The Curious Barista's Guide to Coffee* (2015), *The Curious Bartender's Gin Palace* (2016) and *The Curious Bartender's Rum Revolution* (2017). During the course of his research, Tristan has travelled to over 250 distilleries in over 20 countries, including Holland, Scotland, Mexico, Cuba, France, Lebanon, Italy, Guatemala, Japan, USA and Spain.

Tristan is husband to Laura and father to Dexter and Robin. In his very limited spare time he rides a Triumph motorcycle, takes photos, designs websites, bakes stuff, cooks a lot, attempts various DIY tasks beyond his level of ability, and collects whisky and books.